Wind

The Story of a Wild Horse Rescue

Written and illustrated by
Denise F. Brown,
with her paintings and drawings

Wind, The Story of Wild Horse Rescue

Library of Congress #_____
ISBN-13: 978-1470120948
ISBN-10: 1470120941

This is a work of fiction. Names, characters, places and incidents are
used ficticiously. Any resemblance to actual persons living or dead,
places, events or business establishments is entirely coincidental.

Dedication

To all the wild mustangs
and to Cloud and his herd,
who inspired me to write and illustrate this story.

For all the horse and animal lovers
and rescue organizations
who protect and help the mustangs
in their struggle for survival on and off public lands.

In the hope that future generations
will be able to see them
as living treasures
and love them as much as I do.

Table of Contents

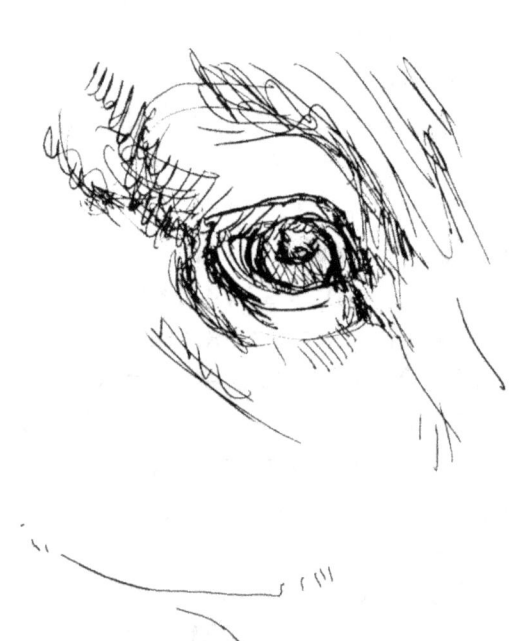

Chapter 1

Wind's Family

I am a wild horse named Wind, but they call me Windy.

I don't mind my name. After all, my mother constantly talks about how my twin sister and I can run like the wind, so the name seems to fit. She is always telling me, "you should be proud of a strong name like Wind, for one day you will become a great stallion, following in the footprints of your ancestors."

She spends hours telling us about one ancestor in particular, called Horsefeathers. I love to listen to all the exciting stories about him and how he escaped from the Spaniards years ago with fifteen mares. This small herd of domestic horses from Europe learned to survive as

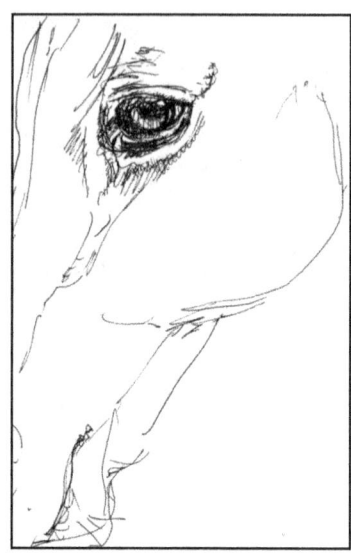

wild horses, searching for fresh water, foraging for food on the plains, and finding shelter in the mountains and canyons. Horsesfeathers' offspring multiplied and divided into many large bands of wild mustangs throughout America. Their descendants are still alive today, including my herd!

My father is a blood relative of Horsefeathers called Silverado. He's a fearless white stallion and is always circling us or standing guard on top of the hill watching for danger. If another stallion or predator comes too close to my family, he will charge and attack them, or chase us away to a safe place hidden in the canyon. He promised, "I will fight to the death to protect my family." He has fought with many stallions, especially one named Rusty, who keeps trying to steal his mares. The intruders end up running away in a bloody mess.

The mares must follow the stallion who wins, so my father has no mercy for any of his opponents.

His lead mare is my mother, Morning Rain. Always alert to my father's commands, she can smell danger just like he can. She loves him very much and would follow him anywhere. If he signals us to run, she is the first mare to scream an alert. She was born on the morning of a torrential rainstorm that washed out half of our valley. She tells us the story of how she and her parents had to run to high ground to escape the flash flooding. She is always afraid of storms.

I love the rain when it washes my back, but it makes Mom very nervous, especially when thunder cracks and lightning strikes too close to us. My father tries to calm her fears by finding shelter for us near the red rocks during dangerous mountain storms. "Avoid the lightning no matter what," my father warns us, "It can kill a horse in an instant!" There are so many things to learn from my father and mother, but being young, it's difficult for me to pay attention all the time.

My twin sister, Stargazer, is happiest when she's chasing butterflies and flirting with the other colts, but I prefer jumping over the rocks and play fighting with the older youngsters from last year's offspring. When the colts get tired of me bothering them they try to bite my neck or rump, but I'm too fast and usually get away. Then I run back toward them and rear up like my father does when he fights with other stallions. My sister just turns her head smiles at me. She knows each play fight will make me stronger and smarter.

I want to be able to protect her when we get older. I tell her, "I'll always look after you, Stargazer, and even fight mountain lions to save you!" She says I'm a little terror. I have battle scars on my light gray coat and even have a scratch on the white blaze down my face to prove it.

One day, an older colt was completely annoyed with me when I couldn't stand still. He kicked my face with his front foot and made me see stars, then chased after me and bit my leg. My mother was very upset with both of us and split us up for the rest of the afternoon.

I don't hate him for kicking me, but sooner or later, I'll grow tall enough to get back at him. We all try to stay friends, as our fights are usually just to impress each other with speed and sure-footed tactics and not to hurt each other badly.

Our mornings and afternoons were spent running and jumping or sleeping and grazing. We gathered together at the end of the day in a place my father felt safe for the night. Before we dozed off to sleep, we often told each other of our tales and adventures.

Chapter 2

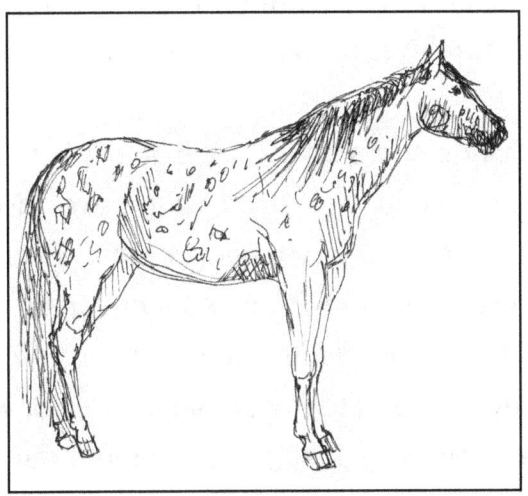

Rocket's Tale of Terror

One true story I will never forget was told by another member of our herd. He's an old black and white spotted gelding named Rocket, who always tags along with us. My father tolerates him, as long as he keeps his distance from the mares and foals. He's not very interested in anything except to eat and stay within the safety of our herd. Rocket told us how he had once been captured by mustangers but they let him go.

My father thinks that the real reason he was set free was that he was too old to work on a ranch anymore. "He's a gelding," he explained. "That means he's been 'fixed' so he can't breed with the mares. The man who owned him abandoned him out in the desert." I didn't really understand what that all meant, but I'm sure that I don't want that to happen to me.

Rocket has strange scars on the left side of his neck. I asked him about it and he told me that the marks are called code numbers. "They stand for when and where I was caught. The cowboys believed they owned me, so they forced me in a squeeze stall and branded my hide with a metal tool. First they shaved my coat and then pushed the tool down hard on my neck. After they were done branding me, I ran out of the stall and shook my head. It didn't really hurt, but I hate the men who marked my beautiful coat forever," he said sadly. "But that's nothing compared to what they did to my mother." Rocket slowly told us about his mother's death.

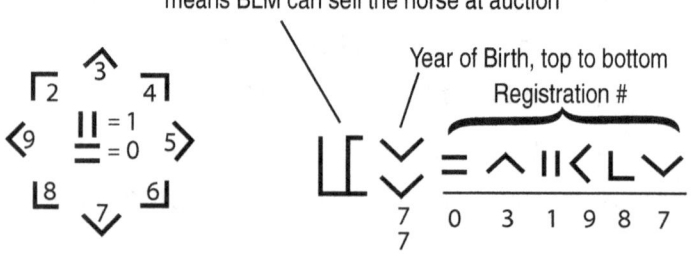

How to read Freeze Brand Marks
Alpha Angle Code

"U" = US Government Registration
means BLM can sell the horse at auction

Year of Birth, top to bottom
Registration #

7
7   0   3   1   9   8   7

Liquid nitrogen is used with a metal tool to brand mustangs.

Arizona
80001-160000

California
160001-240000

Colorado
240001-320000

Idaho
320001-400000

Montana
400001-480000

Nevada
480001-640000

New Mexico
640001-720000

Oregon
0-80000

Utah
720001-800000

Wyoming
800001-880000

Eastern States
880001-880100

"My mother was sold at an auction and taken by truck to a country north of here called Canada. The truck dropped her off at a slaughterhouse. It's a horrible place where they take unwanted horses. She was shot and killed there, and then butchered to be eaten by people." Rocket paused and then continued.

"That's all I know. The horse that told me about all this was rescued from that slaughterhouse and resold at an auction. He ended up on the ranch that I used to live on and he tells all the other horses about what he witnessed at that place."

I shivered. "I don't want to die in a slaughterhouse," I told Rocket after he finished telling us about his mother's horrible fate.

Rocket also has a blue mark on his back. My father said, "He was sprayed with blue paint so he would not be captured again in a roundup." I wondered what a roundup was. It sounded scary and I knew I didn't want any part of that either. "I never want to leave my home!" I exclaimed. "I love the mountains that we live in."

Rocket's news about his mother terrified us, but being youngsters, we shook this off and soon started to run around and play again. It was hard to imagine this ever happening to any of us. We felt so safe here. Besides, I didn't want to think about a slaughterhouse anyway. I had places to explore, and other colts to chase, and the sun was shining brightly. I wandered away from Rocket and back to the grassy hillside with the other colts to explore a bit and look for rabbits.

Chapter 3

No Place Like Home

Running around our meadow makes me feel courageous and as free as the eagles that fly in the sky around the mountain peaks. This is a great place for horses to grow up.

The soft ground almost makes me delirious when I roll on it. It feels so good to lay on our backs and flatten the thick grass that grows as high as my shoulder blades. Fresh mountain air fills my nostrils with wonderful smells like wet grass and sweet mountain flowers. Every member of the herd loves to sleep on the blanket of purple flowers covering the hills in the spring. We are constantly snacking on them and in the summer, the yellow flowers are peppery tasting and delicious to eat.

The spring rain makes the ground smell fresh and clean. We love to roll in the dirt and get caked in mud. When our coats dry off, the layers of dirt keep us cool from the hot sun. My mother believes that it's good for our skin, she said, "Mud baths will keep the horse flies from biting you and helps to heal scratches and bee stings." I told her, "I will roll in the mud more often!"

It's so much fun leaping over the rocks and scrub brush. My father tells us, "Jumping will make your legs grow longer and faster." This comment made us chase each other even more. "I want to grow up strong and brave, just like my father," I thought to myself.

Our lives seem idyllic playing in the shadow of the Great
Red Rock Mountains among the rabbits, prairie dogs and
eagles. There are few worries for me to think about except
how much faster I can run. I love when the sun shines on
my face and warms me up. The light rain and mountain mist
feel refreshing and make the grasses taste so sweet and
irresistible. We graze all day long, unless we are playing
or napping.

But one day, change was in the air. The autumn wind was
getting stronger, blowing constantly through our manes.
Cold weather had triggered our coats to grow longer and
thicker to keep us warm at night. My father explained,
"We need a heavy layer of hair to protect us from the
freezing winter season. I feel it in my bones that the snow
will be here early this year."

Being youngsters, we weren't very concerned and
didn't always pay attention to his comments and
commands. We just ran about, chasing whatever
the wind kicked up through the valley.

I had no idea what changes were about to happen.
The wind was blowing in not just a new season but
a new chapter in my life. This is my story.

Chapter 4

Chased and Rounded Up

The cold and damp fall mornings made the frost on the wet grass very slippery. I chased the other colts and fillies up to the top of the hill which was as far as we were allowed to go by ourselves. We were told by our mothers, "Never go completely out of our site." Since the hilltop was still in range of their vision, we always felt safe with their watchful eyes upon us. We knew they were on constant alert for danger.

We played and kicked our heels at each other for hours until we got tired of all the roughhousing and collapsed onto a nice grassy spot near our mothers. The meadow had turned into golds and reds, making the ground crunchy under me and smelling like dry hay. My eyelids grew heavy as I surrendered to a nice lazy nap in the warm afternoon sun.

Then suddenly, my mother screamed, "Run! Now!" I knew how to run. I had been running since birth. But this day was different. My father pounded his hooves and raced behind us, biting the rumps of our small band of wild horses, yelling "Don't look back until I say we are safe!"

We raced through the canyon and around pinion and juniper trees trees and down a rocky hillside. When we reached the stream bed, father forced us to leap into the fast-flowing water. "You must keep running!" he cried. The stream was bitterly cold but I barely noticed as we galloped over the slippery stones, water splashing our chests.

I turned to look behind and saw strange horses chasing us. They had people on their backs, yelling "Yee Ha! Come on! Move!" The men waved their arms and hats at us. We were so frightened that we didn't notice we had run past the safe zone. We were headed into a small canyon scattered with cactus plants and rocks that we had to jump over. I stumbled a few times as I tried to keep up with everyone.

Near the side of the canyon wall, a horse that I didn't
recognize came out of nowhere. He seemed to know where
he was going. Soon he began leading our entire herd. He
had a strange red rope on his head that none of the other
horses seemed to notice. He commanded, "Follow me!"
I later found out that he was trained to be a "Judas horse."
(Judas means traitor.) He had been taught by a man to
lead other horses towards a holding pen.

So not knowing why or where we were going, all the mares and yearlings followed him hoping to find a safe place to hide. I will never forget how the Judas horse tricked us and I will never forgive him for betraying us!

As we ran down the hill, the air became thick with dust. Loose stones flew past my face. I could hardly see anything in front of me. The Judas horse was leading us closer to the rocks. I didn't understand what was happening.

Suddenly, a great roaring sound came up from around the
boulders that lined the foothills of the mountainside. Then
I saw it, a monstrous flying machine was hovering around
us — a helicopter! It chased us for miles! I was so out of
breath that I thought my lungs and heart would explode.

My tender hoofs hurt. Even though I run and play all day,
I was not used to running for so long without stopping. My
right hoof was bleeding from landing on the sharp rocks and
it began to hurt badly. We ran past a line of metal fences and
into a round pen. Then immediately we all came to a halt.
I was so scared. I couldn't see a way out. This was a trap.

I started to whinny frantically, "Mother, where are you? Please come and find me!" I suddenly realized she was not behind me and my father was not in sight either. I was frightened out of my wits looking for them. I only recognized three other horses from my herd. The rest were not horses that I knew or had ever seen before in our valley. "Who are you?" I neighed as we circled around and around in the pen. The other horses were from different parts of the mountains, but now we were trapped here together.

My mother and father were nowhere to be seen. They seemed to have escaped down a hidden pass after our wild run through the streambed. I wasn't sure where my sister was. Was she trapped like me? Or did she get free? I tried not to panic, as I yelled and screamed until my throat ached, "father, come save me!"

A frenzied mare kicked me in the shoulder as she ran past me around the pen. I was in grave danger with everyone kicking and trying to jump over the walls. There so much panic among the big horses as they crashed into me and stumbled alongside the metal bars!

The noise was almost unbearable. Stallions were fighting with each other and mares were crying and searching for their babies.

I noticed the stallion from another herd called Rusty; he was running in circles around a corral next to me. This big red horse was always fighting with my father and trying to steal mares from our herd. Their vicious battles would last for hours. But now he was trapped and just about crazy with anger to be separated from his lead mare, Dusty.

He was rearing up and kicking his hooves in all directions and shouting out for her, "Dusty, I'll try to jump over the gate to get to you!" He tried to leap over the top, but one of his front feet got stuck in the metal rails of the high fence.

A wrangler ran over to the stallion and touched him on the head with a hotshot stick that sent an electric shock to his face. He immediately lunged back and fell on his side. Rusty struggled so hard to get up, but his neck was broken. The cowboys riding horses dragged him out of the holding pen with ropes and into a truck. I never saw him again, but I could hear his screaming as they took him away, "Dusty! Dusty! I'm hurt. I can't save you anymore."

Seconds later, I heard two shotgun sounds. Then, I heard two more. I froze in my tracks. I couldn't hear Rusty yelling anymore. "Did they shoot him? Will I be shot too?"

I panicked and ran into the metal fence face first. My nose started to bleed. I tried to hide in a corner and not get hurt anymore.

Chapter 5

Captured

𝐴 n old cowboy on the back of a roan colored horse
spotted me. He yelled, "I'm going to take that young one
home with me." Somehow I was snatched up in the air
and put on top of his horse.

Then, just like that, I was thrown into another pen, where
I ran through a narrow chute that was only wide enough for

one adult horse to pass through. I thought I was going to get away, but a man waved a flag on a big long stick at me. He forced me to run up a ramp into a dark enclosed trailer. My eyes bulged with fright when the flag almost touched me. My nostrils were burning red from breathing too fast. "I don't want to be inside here," I cried and tried to kick the cowboy who was shoving me further inside.

I couldn't see the sky anymore. The wooden slats of this cage allowed me to only see glimpses of the mountains. I was trapped inside. "Please don't keep me in here! Let me out!" I cried.

There are some things you just can't imagine will happen.
Being trapped in a trailer was one of them. Smelling the
strong odors of other horses who had been in here only
made me more terrified.

Two men grabbed me; they put a rope around my neck
and looped it around my bleeding nose. "The rope is tied
too tight!" I whimpered. I tried with all my strength to get
away but the other end of the rope was tied to the side
walls. I could hardly turn my head, never mind escape.

"Tie him up tight so he won't hurt his legs," the old man said. I was nearly paralyzed with fear. I couldn't cry for help; I couldn't escape, and my mother was gone.

Chapter 6

The Ground Was Moving

The ground beneath my feet started to shake. The mountains started moving too. I didn't know what was happening. I was scared and felt ill from all the rumbling and movement. I panicked and tried to break away.

I started to jump up, but a cowboy standing next to me was holding my side and neck. I could hardly shift my feet. He yelled, "Whoa, stop it!" He pushed me against the wall and nearly knocked the wind out of my chest. I cried to myself, "Where am I going? Where's my mother?"

The other horses in the trailer were looking at me. I didn't
know them and they didn't smell like wild horses. Then
I realized that one of them was the "Judas horse" who
betrayed my family. I could only stare back at him. I started
to tremble again. I hated him so much. I grumbled under my
breath and promised myself, "Someday I will kick him in the
head if I get the chance."

I didn't know where I was going, but the ground continued
to move under me. The trailer bumped along a dirt road that
my father had always warned us not to play near. He would
tell us, "You will be in danger if you follow that road, so
never go that way!" But here I was, being taken away on
the road I was not supposed to walk on.

I couldn't hear the other wild horses screaming in the holding pens anymore. We were leaving my mountains. They got smaller in the distance. I couldn't even recognize the desert. I kept shivering. It was hard to breathe. The ride went on for several hours.

Then the ground stopped moving. I was so weak. My long skinny legs were shaking and I was dizzy with fear. I didn't know where I was. I felt so alone.

I didn't know why my family could not protect me from
these men. "My mother must be so worried," I thought.
tried hard to listen for her voice and imagined her
crying out for me, "Windy, my son, where are you?"

Chapter 7

Arrival at the Ranch

People were peeking through the slats of the trailer to look at me. I could hear talking but didn't understand all that they said. A young girl named Emily reached her hand in to touch my ear. I tried to bolt away but could not. "Don't touch me!" I whinnied and tried to scare her away, but it was me that was afraid. My heart was pounding.

I thought I was going to die from fright. My throat was dry as dust and I choked and coughed. Somehow I needed to escape and run back to my family.

Suddenly, the door of the trailer opened. "Come on out,"
a man said. He pushed my hind quarters to force me out
while another cowboy held my head and jerked the rope
around my neck. I jumped out of the trailer and ran down
the ramp. There were tall fences everywhere. I couldn't
get away.

Chapter 8

Locked in the Barn

I heard a loud whinny from another horse in the yard. The old man, who everyone called Grampa, said, "Let's put Seashell in the barn next to the colt. If we're lucky, Seashell might adopt him, then he won't miss his mother so much."

Stan Brown, who everyone called "Grampa," had been riding horses his whole life. He grew up on a cattle ranch and heard stories from his grandfather of the wild horses who raced through the nearby canyons. As a young cowboy, he had heard other cowboys grumble about these wild

horses and their fears that they were using up land and resources needed for their cows. But Grampa never quite bought into that way of thinking. The horses were here first; they were part of the range. It seemed that both cattle and horses should have their place. And so, though he hated the mustang roundups, he found himself there each year — buying what horses he could afford in an effort to save them.

The young girl called Emily said, "I'm going to sleep in the barn tonight. I'll try to think of a good name for this little fellah. Maybe I'll call him Windy; I bet he runs like the wind."

Grampa added, "He does run like the wind. That'll be a good name for him."

As she walked toward me, Emily spoke softly, "You poor
little guy. You really are scared — especially after getting
separated from your mother and going on such a long ride.
You must be thirsty. I'll get a bucket of water and some fresh
hay for you. You can have a good supper and a nice sleep."

I watched Emily as she filled the pail of water. She was
slender with long, blonde hair the color of my mother's
mane and tail. A red ribbon tied it back. She spoke softly
but everything was so strange to me. I was too afraid to
listen. "I miss my mother and my family, and I'm so tired.
Please let me go!" I neighed.

My front hoof was chipped and my shoulder still hurt from being kicked by the mare in the holding pen. I just wanted to collapse and sleep through this bad dream. "I hope I'll wake up in our field in the mountains," I sighed. "My mother will be near me, and my father will be standing guard."

I stumbled. Someone picked me up and carried me into the barn. I had no more strength to fight. They put me in the corner of a dusty, dark stall. "There you go, Windy," said the old cowboy, "Sleep tight, don't let the bed bugs bite."

I looked up as they walked away from me and then at the ground. "What are bed bugs? What is a bed?" I worried about where I was. My whole body felt weak. I finally fell asleep on a hard wooden floor that smelled of urine and manure.

Grampa said, "Come in the house, Emily. He will still be there in the morning."

Chapter 9

Morning After Captured

A crazy rooster was yelling his head off, "Wake up! Get up! It's morning." I woke to the stark reality that I was not dreaming. I was alone in a dark stall far away from my home. The old horse in the stall next to me was watching me like my mother does. She tried to nuzzle me and push her nose through the opening in the wooden slats. Smelling her, I felt a little less nervous.

"They call me Seashell," she nickered.

"I have never talked to another horse before who was not part of my herd," I told her. "My father would not allow it." I was relieved to realize she meant me no harm. I felt a little safer when she said, "You can stand next to me if you want to."

Horses don't like to be alone. We feel safer in groups and protected from predators like mountain lions or bears when the herd's many eyes watch out for each other. My father

depended on the whole herd to be on alert for any signs of danger. If any noise or scent alarmed my family, we would run to higher ground or through the canyon to one of our hideouts. We could then graze and play without fear from any harm...except for yesterday, when the men on horses and the flying monster chased us out of our mountain valley home.

"My father told me never to go near people or where they live," I said to Seashell. "He said that your freedom will be lost forever. They'll trick you and trap you in a pen ane even burn brand marks onto your hide. They might even sell you to a rodeo or to a slaughterhouse and eat you." My mind was racing again. I wanted to go home to my herd.

Seashell just sighed, "Don't worry, you are safe here now with me."

The barn was musty with hay and horse odors. I was used to fresh air, open skies and clean ground. The stall that locked me in didn't have a window so I couldn't see the mountains. "I want to go home," I cried to Seashell and the other horses.

A sorrel colored mare peaked her head out of the stall across from me. "We live here and like being fed twice a day," she said. "We get oats and hay and plenty of water."

"Everything is different from my life in the wild," I said. I saw people walking around carrying ropes and buckets, and there were dogs barking outside in the yard. "They might chase me, too," I thought. I heard cows mooing and lots of chickens making strange cackling sounds.

"It's so noisy here," I complained. Seashell tried to console me, "It's normal for all of the yelling and people talking loudly at the ranch." I tried to relax a tiny bit and stop being scared.

A loud rumble shook the wall near me. The big barn door opened and I began to shake and felt frightened all over again. The old cowboy was entering the barn with another hired hand.

"What now?" I thought. I stomped my foot on the wooden floor and whinnied. "Why am I hear?!" They didn't pay any attention to me. They each just grabbed a saddle and walked back out of the barn. I was relieved that they left me alone.

Chapter 10

Why the Roundup?

A winter storm was approaching. It would cover the land with heavy, deep snow as high as a horse. This bad weather was the reason for the roundup that caught me. I heard Emily and Grampa talking about how the land management people feared that the wild horses would starve during the winter if some of us weren't rounded up and removed from the territory.

Grampa and one of his older ranch hands were heading over to the horse barn. "I don't understand why so many cattle ranchers want to get rid of the few remaining mustangs. The cattle outnumber horses on public land between 100-400 cows to one horse." muttered Slate. "Some ranchers even put out baited poison traps and fence them out of watering holes to kill them."

"Yeah, they think they're just pests grazing in cattle country. They want them to be taken off the land so the cows can eat up all the grass," said Tom, another one of Grampa's hired hands. "If the herds continue to be thinned out, the wild horses will be extinct within a few years."

Grampa added, "I've read that some naturalists even believe that already there's not enough healthy stock to sustain the wild herd's gene pool. Horse families are being broken up and sent away to live in holding pens or to be auctioned off and adopted. Thousands of wild horses are sent to slaughterhouses in Canada and Mexico. They end up in Europe and Japan as horse meat...for people to eat! It's just not right." Grampa grumbled and shook his head, "But that's a whole other bad story." He sighed, "Those animals taken to be slaughtered are incredibly abused and mistreated. I can't bear to talk about it."

Tom added, "Horses are transported over the border to Canada at many crossing points, even in states as far away as Maine. The horses must be healthy enough for human consumption. And even worse, if a sick horse on its way to Mexico is not acceptable for slaughter, they set it free in the desert with no water or food and is left all alone to die of dehydration."

Emily joined them in time to hear Grampa's last remark. "If their is evil in this world, then inhumane treatment of horses is an example of it," she said.

Grampa said, "There are so many sides to the slaughter debate. The pro-slaughter people say there are too many unwanted horses and slaughter is the only way to control the population. They make a living selling horses to slaughterhouses in price per pound of horse meat."

"What kind of people would want to work there anyway! I don't know anyone who would like that job. It would be better to euthanize a horse then put them through that kind of hell on earth," Tom added. "Horses are tougher to kill that other animals that are slaughtered. Their brain is set back further in their skull. Some are still conscious after the stungun shot knocks them down and are just butchered still alive."

"Any horse sold at auction, even if it was once somebody's beloved pet, is just one bad sale away from the bloody slaughterhouse floor. Slaughter needs to be banned completely," Emily said.

Grampa replied, "Some people against horse slaughter are advocates for responsible breeding and mandatory horse registration in order to limit the number of unwanted horses. Then, there are the naturalists who believe in the law of nature and natural selection and say the wild horse's characteristics and traits will be lost forever with a selective breeding program."

"It's a dilemma for the people who manage the wild horse population on the public lands. The land management bureau doesn't want to listen to anybody else. They seem to think they own the public land instead of the taxpayer."

Tom added, "Oil drillers and miners want to get rid of the mustangs, too. They can make huge profits by using the National Parks land in ways other than what it was set aside for."

"Even though legislation was passed to allow wild horses and wild burros to live freely and be protected, it's difficult to enforce these laws," said Grampa. "Unfortunately, the debate always ends up in the hands of politicians who vote-in legislation that isn't strong enough to protect the wild horse population."

"People have to speak up before the BLM castrates or kills all the stallions. Putting geldings back in the herds just causes trouble. Most of them still try to fight with the stallions and break up healthy bands of horses, even though they can't breed with the mares.

Grampa thought about the current bill in Congress, called HR 2966, the American Horse Slaughter Prevention Act of 2011, that would prohibit horse slaughter in the United States and make the shipping of horses to other countries illegal. "The pro-slaughter side is fueled by big money from pro-slaughter businesses like beef and oil companies. It'll be difficult to win such a dirty fight. Using tax dollars to fund this inhumane and controversial practice is a not what most Americans agree with today," said Grampa.

Grampa lifted a fresh bucket of water over the door and into my stall. He huffed a bit and said, "Well, luckily for this little guy, not everyone believes in the "thinning the herd" strategy. New legislation is in the works to be voted on in Washington to help preserve the wild horse herds in protected areas of the West."

Then he added, "The wild horse is symbolic of the American spirit. They shouldn't be taken from the lands where they have roamed free for centuries. It's hard to believe that 100,000 American horses are exported for slaughter each year."

"Yeah, public outcry to save the mustangs is growing across the country and around the world," said Sharpie, another of Grampa's hired hands. "Washington is going to have to decide how to protect the horses before time runs out. Their extinction will be a tragedy because of corrupt land management profiteers," said Sharpie. "It's an *equine holocaust* if you ask me."

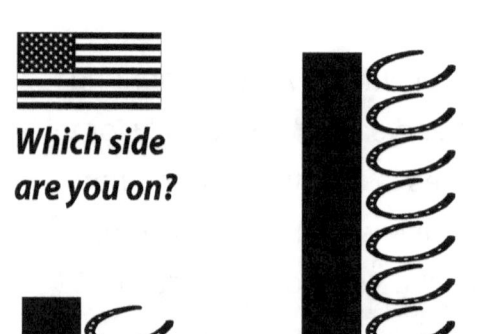

Which side are you on?

80% of the American public is opposed to horse slaughter for human consumption within the United States.

"People need to speak up and tell the government that horse slaughter and cruel treatment of horses must be stopped," said Emily. "Kids in school are writing letters to Washington. I'm going to write to my Congressman and the President of the United States. Dad can add a link to the ranch's website — maybe with a sample letter. I wonder if the President's kids will write him a letter too?"

"The Internet will make it easy for people to join the fight. Kids can spread the word on their cell phones and computers. We need to tell everyone to support the American Horse Slaughter Prevention Act (H.R. 2966 and S. 1176). It will stop the sale and transportation of horses for slaughter in the United States, and keep horses from being taken across the borders to Canada and Mexico."

Dear Mr. President Obama

Please save the wild horses before it is too late...

Sincerely,

American public opinion

http://www.whitehouse.gov

The White House
1600 Pennsylvania Avenue NW
Washington, DC 20500

I didn't really understand what they were talking about, but it sounded serious. I knew it related to me somehow when they walked over and looked at me in my stall. I tried to hide in the corner.

Then Grampa reached out his hand to me. "Don't touch me," I whinnied, as I backed up further into the corner to get away from his hand. "Tell me where I am and why did you bring me here?" I thought to myself. There were so many questions running through my mind that did not make any sense to me.

I had trouble sleeping that night after thinking about what the men talked about. I remembered Rocket's mother's death in the slaughterhouse. My dreams turned terrifying as I envisioned my mother being taken away. I woke up trembling, fearful of what my future might hold at this ranch.

Chapter 11

King Ranch

I had actually been brought to a special place called King Ranch. It covers 4,000 acres of open range which is mostly scrub country filled with plenty of cacti, rattlesnakes and prairie dogs. It's not a cattle ranch. It's a wild horse rescue sanctuary that also takes in other animals in need.

One hundred years ago, two million wild horses roamed the American West. Today there are less than 35,000. Grampa's vision was to do what ever he could to protect the small population that is left in the whole country.

Recently, several livestock misfits were brought here — two little wild burros named Jake and Jacques that were captured near the Grand Canyon, an old zebra, called Stripes, who was from a zoo that closed down, and several adopted wild horses that their owners couldn't handle.

These animals had been given a chance to live out their life on this ranch with plenty of food and water. They seemed happy and at peace in the big field next to the round corral. There was a huge water trough and piles of hay for them on the ground. Emily's father, Jim, is working on a solar powered water pump for the wild horses. He plans to set up a pump in the foothills for the horses on the range.

"I'm not a misfit," I screamed. "I have a family of my own." I protested by stomping my feet and rearing up on my hind legs. I was so angry. I was ready to bite anyone if they came near me. At the time, I did not feel kindly toward Grampa or Emily.

Chapter 12

Grampa Brown

For decades, ranch owners of King Ranch and other ranches throughout the West needed plenty of horses for work and transportation. The ranch hands got excited to saddle up and ride in the roundups. They would pick the strongest and best looking horses to keep for themselves and sell the extra ones to auctions or rodeos.

This year, Grampa didn't ride in the roundup. He used to love to catch wild horses, but he didn't have the flexibility of a young man anymore to sit in saddle all day. Old age and arthritis had settled into his bones.

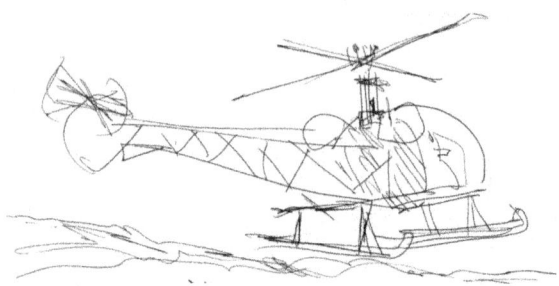

Grampa said, "In the old days, we'd ride horses to roundup mustangs. Now, it's easier to hire a pilot to chase the horses by helicopter. It's bad for the horses though. They're forced to run for too long and too fast in the hot sun. The horses and burros overheat and hyperventilate. Their hooves get beat up and some of 'em go lame or break a leg. Then they're no good to anyone and have to be shot.'

"I've seen little foals who can't keep up with their mothers collapse and fine stallions go crazy trying to protect their families. I just don't understand how people who say they wanna help horses allow this to happen."

"People don't realize that the stress makes their brains almost fry and shoots their metabolism through the roof. It can damage their hearts and lungs. Some mares even abort their babies when they get to the corral from all the running and exhaustion. Their bodies just can't take it. It's bad horse management."

Grampa thought about all those years in the saddle. Yes, he would have regrets, but his rocking chair didn't look too bad these days either. It sat on the back porch where the sunsets were best. Grampa would strum his guitar and sing to the dogs who wailed in accompaniment. And while he played, he would think of what needed to be done to save the wild horses.

Chapter 13

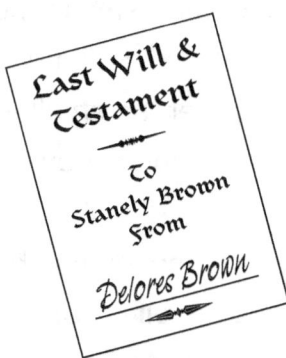

Grampa's Wish to Help Mustangs

R escuing wild horses was not originally Grampa's idea —
it came from his twin sister, Delores, who passed away a
few years earlier at the age of 75. Delores, Emily's great
aunt, loved horses and rode them during her vacations at
the ranch. She had never owned one herself because she
lived in the city. When she was young, Delores travelled
east to go to college, and wound up staying in Boston.
She built a successful advertising agency and became a
wonderful artist.

Her favorite subject was horses and she drew and painted
them whenever she had time. When her husband died,
Delores made out her will and decided her estate should
go to Grampa, with one stipulation: Use her money to turn
his ranch into a wild horse sanctuary. When Delores died,
Grampa complied and King Ranch was born.

Grampa had owned cattle for many years but in recent times it had become hard for a small ranch to make money. He hated to do it, but finally sold off much of his big herd. Big business was taking over the smaller ranches and he couldn't keep up with taxes and expenses.

When he received Delores money and her instructions to start a rescue sanctuary, he felt it was a "gift from Heaven." Right then and there, he made up his mind to carry out her wishes. "This is a fight that will change the West again," he said. "There is a lot of work to be done — legislation to change, laws to correct. It's a life-and-death fight for survival for the remaining wild horse herds and I aim to make sure it's a fight they win."

At first, it wasn't easy to convince some of his old friends about his plan. Grampa had worked for the Bureau of Land Management (the BLM) when he was younger, and the guys he worked with had mixed feelings about wild horses. "Why would anyone want to save them? Mustangs eat all the grassland that the cattle graze on and they just multiply too darn fast," some of them said when he talked about his decision to change the ranch. "They're a nuisance! They're like feral cats. You might as well poison 'em all."

Grampa tried to explain, "I've seen a lot of abuse and bad treatment to the wild horses on the roundups, but was never really able to do much to stop anything. Now's my opportunity to make amends to mustangs. It's all about money and survival of the fittest when it comes down to the land, cattle and wild animals," he said.

His friends still argued that mining and oil drilling were a more profitable use of the land, but Grampa stood firm. He knew that either of these options and greed would mean the end of the wild horse herds.

Changing the minds of these ranchers will be a challenge. "Wild mustangs are living treasures, not just horses in the movies," he told them.

King Ranch was now part of the "new deal" to change the laws and protect the wild herds from being captured and thinned out. Grampa believed it would actually cost less to leave the wild horses free on the public lands and provide feed and water then to capture and hold them prisoners in corrals for years.

"If the captured horses aren't adopted within 10 years, they go to a slaughterhouse," he explained to Emily. "They're miserable being corralled and in the end, far too many wind up as a horse steak or burger on dinner tables in Japan and Europe."

Tom nodded. "The life of a horse stuck in a stockyard is not a good one. The horses have been torn from their families. They're crammed into holding pens with no shade or protection from snow, rain or wind. They can't run. The pregnant mares birth their foals on the filthy dirt. It's a tragedy for an animal born to be free."

"I was a cattleman for years," said Grampa. "But cattle don't need to eat up every acre of grass out there. We need new legislation to protect these animals. There are millions of acres of open land suitable for horse herds; there are places for them to live free and die free as intended. If only all Americans knew what was happening to our wild horse population they would be shocked — and more steps would be taken to help them."

Tom shook his head and said, "The horses and burros should be allowed to live on the range where they don't cost anything, just as the US Congress voted UNANIMOUSLY to do back in 1971."

The dinner bell began to ring noisily from the house porch. "Let's go, y'all. It's time to eat. Beef stew and Pat's blue ribbon apple pie are on the menu!" The cowboys liked sitting in the fresh air so meals were served on the picnic tables outside and Emily's mother, Pat, was happy their boots didn't mess up her clean kitchen floor. Grampa smiled at me and said "See ya tomorrow, Windy."

The cowboys asked Pat about horse meat. She said, "Years ago, horse meat was banned in pet food. It's funny, fancy Europeans and Japanese love to eat it. Maybe it's low in fat, but it's tainted with vaccines, pain killers and dewormers. It's taboo, and it sure ain't health food. There's no USDA approved horse meat coming out of Canada and Mexico! Don't worry, there's no horse meat in my beef stew or apple pie. Eat up everybody."

Chapter 14

Hay for Breakfast

Early the next morning, I could hear someone walking toward the barn and a dog barking. The rooster had already crowed. "Now what?" I thought, as the old barn door with the rusty hinge rolled open and Grampa stood in the entrance.

"Well, this little guy certainly needs a safe place to live for the time being," said Gramps as he opened the stall door and stepped in. To my disappointment, he closed the door behind him.

He stood very still as he looked me over. His voice was quiet when he said, "Maybe someday we can return you to your family, but for now, we have to put some meat on those skinny ribs and long legs. So, you'll just have to put up with us and live here for the winter. Old Seashell will watch out for you. Now get some rest and try to eat your breakfast."

He threw some fresh hay down. I jumped four feet in the air and spun around in a circle. I wanted to be free and run outside. "I never ate baled hay before and I'm not going to start now!" I squealed. I tried to bite the wooden stall door. Seashell said, "Better not do that. Cribbing will break your teeth. They'll put a collar on your neck that hurts if you keep biting the wood." I told her, "OK, I'll stop it."

I soon realized that I wasn't going to going free anytime soon. The wind started howling and snow was blowing in through the barn windows and doors. "I knew I must rest. Maybe tomorrow the stall door would open again and I could escape."

Chapter 15

The Girl Called Emily

The young girl named Emily stuck her head through the stall gate. "Windy, you are so cute," she whispered. "We're going to become great friends, you'll see." She slowly pushed an apple towards me with her bare hand. The apple smelled good, but I didn't want to accept something from this strange person. Maybe she would drop it on the ground and I could eat it later.

Finally, the apple dropped out of her hand and rolled onto the hay next to me. Emily backed away from the stall, still watching me with her blue eyes. She stood quietly near the door and then turned to go do her chores. I wished that she would leave the door open, so I could jump out of the stall and run away. That didn't happen as Emily knew better than to leave a door open around here.

Emily's mother, Pat, is Grampa's daughter. Emily and her parents have been living on the ranch for six months. They moved in after Grampa told them he needed help with the rescue animals. "Someday you'll inherit this ranch and it's time for you to understand what's happening here," he explained. "I want you to believe in it as much as I and your Great Aunt Delores did."

They were thrilled to be part of the plan, especially Emily. She couldn't wait to move in. She told Grampa, "I'll start working for you immediately, for free!"

Pat became "head cook and bottle washer" and Emily's father, Jim, was web guru and "Mr. Fix It Handyman." Emily was "Barn Maintenance Technician and Horse Namer". In other words, she cleaned stalls, swept the barn, polished saddles, and named all the mustangs. She even nicknamed the ranch "The Peaceable Kingdom," because everyone got along so well.

Gramps knew Emily was the ranch's future. She needed to learn everything about it, including the hard work.

"That's fantastic, Emily," said Grampa, "Your Great Aunt Delores would be so proud. Your generation and children in schools will be responsible for the future of the American mustang. There'll always be a need for a watchdog to oversee the BLM and contact the government if there are any abuses or trouble to report."

Emily was one of those kids people call "horse crazy" who read every horse book and watched all the horse movies. Posters of horses were on her bedroom walls. and each birthday meant another painted pony sculpture for her collection.

Living on the ranch was just magical to her. Regardless of the endless chores, Emily vowed to never complain. She loved all of the animals here, especially old Seashell. Now she was falling in love with the little colt named Wind.

Chapter 16

Seashell, a Fiord Draft Horse

Seashell nickered softly to me so I approached her stall.
I felt safer near the big mare. She was my only comfort
now. I resigned to stop searching around and behind me
for any sign of my mother.

I asked her, "How did you get to this place?" Her coat was
a sandy cream color and she had a white mane which
stood straight up. She had a black stripe that ran along
the top of her back.

She told me, "I'm a Fiord draft horse. My ancestors are from a far away place called the Netherlands, a land near the ocean. They call me Seashell because my hooves are the color of seashells from my home country. They're shiny and multicolored with pinks, blues, gray and tan. When I became lame after a fall two years ago, my owners retired me and brought me here."

"I hope I don't have to stay here that long," I said. "I want to go back to my mountains and family soon." I started to sniffle a bit at the thought of being here for years.

Seashell said, "Windy, please don't keep crying. The people are nice to the animals here. They especially like horses. I don't have to pull wagons or work anymore. They feed us and brush our coats and we always have plenty of water to drink. It's warm in my stall and if the weather gets really cold, they throw a blanket on my back."

"I have a really thick coat that my father said will help me stay warm in the cold winter wind," I said. "I don't need or want a smelly old blanket!"

Morning turned into afternoon and my stomach started to growl. I hadn't eaten since yesterday morning. I decided to eat the apple in my stall. I said to Seashell,"I need to rest. I'll take a nap and dream about my home and my family."

We could hear Grampa singing a song, "Home, home on the range, where the deer and the antelope play; where seldom is heard a discouraging word, and the skies are not cloudy all day...Home, home on the range..." His old dog JoJo started howling back at him. Their singing made me drowsy. My eyes started to close and I fell asleep as the orange sun settled into night.

Chapter 17

Winter Turned into Spring

Time passed slowly as the winter snows turned into spring rains. I learned to eat hay and oats and drink out of a black plastic bucket. There was a back door to my stall that Emily opened for me so I could go outside every day and run around in the corral. Seashell always went outside and stayed near me. We became inseparable.

However, it took Grampa a few weeks to get close to me.
Every time he tried to come near me, I ran away from him.
Finally one day, he caught me off guard while I was day
dreaming and gazing at the mountains. He quickly put a
halter around my head and buckled it up. I froze with fear.
Could I still breathe? It didn't hurt, but it tickled my nose
and I shook my head trying to get it to fall off, but it
wouldn't budge. "He tricked me!" I said to Seashell.
"Why did he put that on me?"

Seashell said, "Don't worry, you'll get used to it. All the
horses at the ranch wear a halter. It's much better than a
bridle with a metal bit. A bit hurts your mouth and can
break your teeth if you chew on the metal too much.

Men use bridles and reins to control us when they want to ride on our back or make us work. They think we don't mind it, but I never liked a piece of cold metal across my tongue. It's uncomfortable and makes me lose my concentration when I'm running. Sometimes, I used to just stop in my tracks because it hurt my old teeth so much. Then my rider would get angry with me and kick the side of my ribs with boots and sharp spurs.

Some people can be very mean to horses. One cart driver even used a whip on my back and yelled curses at me all the time to go faster," she mumbled as she munched on dry hay, "But, not here. They want us to be happy."

Seashell said, "Emily is my favorite human friend. She shows us how much she loves us by giving us treats. She always has an apple or a carrot in her backpack."

We were faithfully visited by Emily every day. She would sit for hours watching me and telling me tales of race horses like Sea Biscuit and Secretariat and movie horses called Hidalgo and the Black Stallion. She told us, "Horses have always been an important part of history. They've worked for man on farms dragging plows, in wars hauling guns, in cities pulling carts, and best of all, as pleasure riding and competing in events called dressage and the grand prix. Champion horses compete in the Olympics all over the world!"

I never knew I had so many famous ancestors like General Robert E. Lee's horse, Traveler, and Paul Revere's horse, Brown Beauty, who took him on his famous ride. Emily knew about them all. She said, "Tomorrow, I'll to tell you my favorite short story about animals and people becoming trusted friends."

LEXINGTON

BOSTON

CONCORD

ARLINGTON

Paul Revere's famous ride —
"The British are coming!"
he cried.

Chapter 18

Nana's Story

The next day, Emily sat on a bale of hay in my stall and read her favorite book to me, written by her own Nana. "It goes like this," Emily said.

"One sunny morning, two children went for a walk on the little path in the woods behind their house. Their cat followed them and they came upon a beautiful wild horse along the trail who started to follow them, too. Then a raccoon started to follow the horse, who was joined by a gray squirrel, then a hummingbird flew along with them; and finally, a green garter snake slid alongside the trail after them.

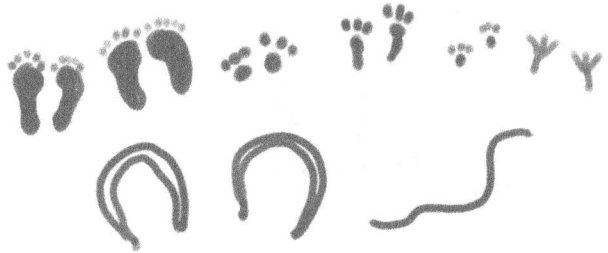

They all walked to a small brook and stopped for a drink of cold water. They were happy to spend time together and became friends. Many different kinds of tracks were left in the sand near the brook that day."

"The children started to walk back home and all the animals followed along until they reached the place where they each met. The snake wiggled his tail as he said 'good-bye'. The bird moved her wing; the squirrel flicked his tail and ran to his nest. The raccoon batted the air with his paws and the horse shook her head good-bye until they met again."

"The children and their cat went home and told their grandmother, who laughed and said, 'Now eat your supper and off to sleep.' They closed their eyes and dreamed about their new friends. The end," said Emily.

"Someday I will write a story about you, Windy!" she said. "Everyone will love to read about your life's story and your great adventures."

I thought about Emily's story and how it reminded me of many of my animal friends back home and a little brook where I often sipped water. I was sad again because I missed my home.

I tried to convince myself to be happy. I was okay for now and I was safe with Seashell. But deep in my heart all I wished was for Grampa to take me back to the mountains when summer returned. I wanted to follow the rabbits along the trail and watch the birds fly above me.

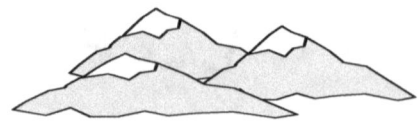

Chapter 19

A Year Later at the Ranch

Summer went by. "The laws are being voted on in Washington that offer more protection to the mustangs," said Grampa."There will be no more roundups after this last one scheduled for October."

October arrived and the last legal roundup in the United States took place. Twenty wild horses were captured that day. One of the horses was brought to the King Ranch. She looked so familiar. It was my sister! I was so excited that I jumped over the corral fence and ran to greet her. I yelled, "Stargazer, it's me, your brother, Wind!"

She was so frightened that she tried to bolt away and run. Finally she recognized me and sniffed my nose. It was a miracle that we were together again.

She was very confused and asked me, "Windy, where have you been? Mother and father thought you were killed in the roundup. So many horses from our herd were caught. I've missed you so badly. We searched for you everywhere. Old Rocket broke his leg when the helicopter tried to chase him away from the corrals. The pilot tried to hurry Rocket and bumped him on his back with the helicopter skid. Rocket panicked and tripped on the rocks from exhaustion. He broke his front leg. Then a cowboy shot him."

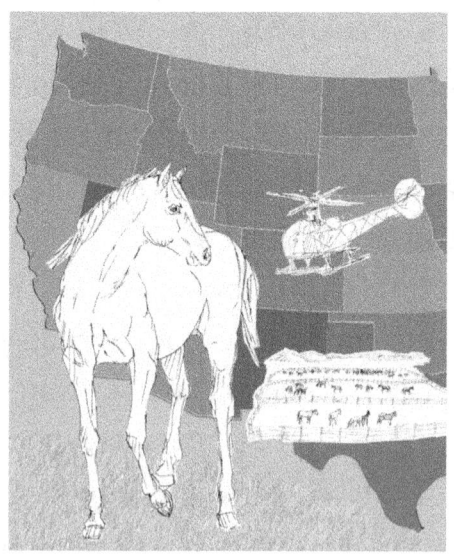

"Oh no! Poor Rocket!" I cried. "I think I heard the rifle shot that killed him. They also shot the big stallion called Rusty. I was afraid they'd shoot me, too." I thought about my old friend, Rocket. "At least Rocket didn't have to die in the slaughterhouse like his mother," I said.

My sister said, "We have been so sad since that day. Father said that life is hard for mustangs. We must always watch out for each other."

She explained that she and our parents escaped through a crack in the canyon that day. But the helicopter came back yesterday and the roundup started again the same way. The herd ran for their lives. "Our father escaped over the hill but mother was nowhere to be seen." "Maybe she hid near the waterfalls," I said, hopefully. We both wished she would be able to find her way back to our father.

I told Stargazer, "You will be safe here with me. Someday we will get to go home together."

Then I pushed her shoulder, "Now, you must meet Seashell. She is my best friend at the ranch." So Stargazer and I spent the afternoon telling Seashell all about our home and family.

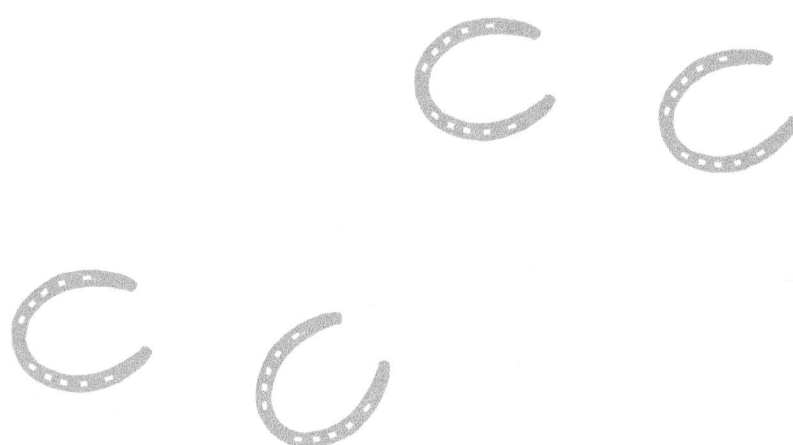

Grampa decided to not train either my sister or I
to be riding horses. He said, "No horseshoes, no
bridles; I don't even want anyone brushing their
coats." He planned to release us someday and
wanted us to remain wild. Emily did what Grampa
wished, even though she wanted to brush the mud
that was caked on our coats. "You always manage to
roll in the stinky mud!" she said. "At least it will help
keep the horseflies away." I thought of my mother
telling me the same thing.

I was glad that no man tried to get on my back and try
to ride me. The thought of a saddle made from dead
cow hides being strapped onto my back gave me the
creeps. I don't like dead animal parts near me.

I learned that many of the rescued horses who came to the ranch had been trained in horse clinics. Some trainers are tough on horses and believe in a heavy hand where strength and dominance are the only way to handle a mustang. If the horse did not behave, some men used whips on them. If that did not work, the 'bad' horses were sent to rodeos and punished with electric prods called hotshots; or worse, their life ended at a slaughterhouse.

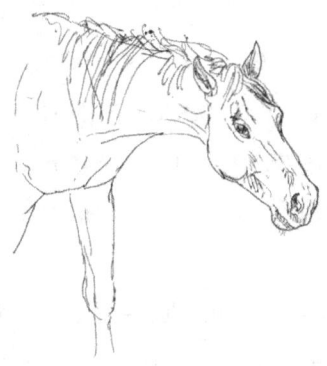

However, a new generation of wild horse trainers believe that a gentler touch and softer voice will win over our trust. They try to understand each horse's personality and build a strong bond of respect between both horse and man.

The other horses told us of "horse whisperers," people who truly love the mustangs and all horses. They have an almost magical way with horses and encourage a slower process of training. They believe in kindness and instead of using prods and whips, primarily use voice commands and touch. I've heard it could be the future of horse training; I hope that is so.

I was pleased to hear Tom say, "If you have to motivate a horse to move, the slight touch of a rope will do the trick. You don't have to beat him over the head. Most bad horses become 'bad' because a person didn't train them correctly. Unless something is wrong with a horse, I blame the trainer first for most of their problems."

The King Ranch was all about "change for the better," for the mustangs, so only trainers who used the new methods were allowed to work here. I was relieved to hear that no horse would be abused or neglected.

The only human touch my sister and I felt was when the veterinarian came to the ranch to examine the livestock and give vaccines. I hated getting shots so when I smelled that man I ran away until they finally forced me into an enclosed and gated stall with metal rails. They said I needed to be put in this "squeeze stall". It had a wall that they pushed in next to me until I couldn't move. They reached in and vaccinated me and took a few samples of my blood to test for diseases.

Luckily, it was over in a few minutes. I ran back to my sister, Stargazer and my friend, Seashell.

I also remember the man with a white collar who was very
kind and soft spoken. The horses tell me that one day
each year he visits the ranch and blesses all the animals.
I'm not sure what that means, but on the day he was here,
everyone stopped in their tracks for a moment of silence.
Even the chickens seem to quiet down and stay still.

"God bless all of your creatures here at this rescue
sanctuary. We are all part of God's creation," he said.
He looked at me and prayed that I would stay safe and
live a long life. Then he left us to visit other ranches down
the road. I wondered if his prayers would help me if I ever
escape from here.

Chapter 20

The Laws Changed

My second long winter at the ranch turned into spring again. With it came good news when a letter arrived one morning. Grampa found out his dream of protecting the wild horses was coming true.

He announced, "New legislation was written and signed by the President of the United States. It is now official that the Bureau of Land Management will stop harvesting wild horses from the government protected lands. It was also passed that mining and oil drilling would not be allowed in America's national parks! Plus, transporting American horses to the slaughterhouses in Canada and Mexico is now illegal."

He clapped his hands above his head and breathed a sigh of relief. "This is a great day for mustangs!" he declared.

The new laws ordered that wild horses would no longer be captured and taken away from their families. Grampa said, "I guess that it's safe to return the wild ones to their home in the mountains. They can have their freedom back and be living treasures like they should be."

Chapter 21

Back to the Mountains

A t the crack of dawn one spring morning that old
rooster woke me up for the last time. Grampa said,
"I think it is safe to return the wild ones to their home
in the mountains. Now they can live free like nature
intended."

The roads where not too muddy for the trucks and the weather report called for clear skies. However, I didn't know what was going on. There were lots of people running around in the yard. Trucks and vans started backing up and noisy ramps opened behind the trailers. When everything was ready, Grampa and the cowboys came to get us. One by one, they walked four horses into the two vans. A young black filly and a white mare were loaded in the first van. The other one was for my sister and me.

I was frightened about going into the van. I didn't have a good experience the last time I walked up a ramp. Somehow, Stargazer was already in there and shouting to me, "Wind! Help me! Where are we going now?!"

It took a lot of coaxing to get me in there, but I wanted to get to my sister. "She needed me!" I thought, so, I finally ran up the ramp. I started to slip sideways, but I stopped myself from falling, and stumbled inside. The cowboy quickly snapped a rope on my halter so I could not get out.

My mom yelled from the porch, "Dinner will be ready when you get back home tonight. I'm making your favorite raspberry pie, Emily." She knew how sad everyone would be tonight after setting us free. Emily says I'm her favorite mustang. Emily took hundreds of photos of me with her camera. She told me she puts them on a website. I didn't know what a website is, but as long as she didn't catch me in a web and hurt me, then it was ok with me.

Then the ground started moving beneath our feet.
"Not again!" I neighed. It was very confusing to see
the ranch getting smaller in the distance as we were
carried down the road. I looked around and screamed,
"Where is Seashell?!" But she was back in the barn.

"I didn't get to say goodbye to my friend," I thought
sadly. "She'll miss me as much as I already miss her."
I put my head down. I wished she could have met my
family. I was very upset to think I might never see her
again, but I realized that she was safe and happy at
the ranch.

After a couple hours riding down the bumpy road, my sister started to neigh with excitement. "Wind, smell the wind blowing outside! It is coming from the mountains! I remember the scent of the purple flowers in the spring! We're near home!"

"We are going to be set free!" I screamed joyfully. Grampa and Emily were keeping their promise. The foothills were in sight.

We wore our halters for the last time. While we were standing in the vans, Emily took each halter off our heads one by one, and kissed our faces. "I'll miss you the most, Windy. You are my best friend," she said as tears streamed down her face. "When I hear the wind in the mountains, I will think of you!"

She gave each one of us a carrot. She tried to delay saying goodbye. Slowly, each horse jumped out of the van and was set free!

Grampa waved us off. "Go have a happy life my friends! You belong to the mountains, running free as the wind!"

The four of us started to run towards the meadow when we glimpsed a small band of wild horses. It was my father, Silverado, and his herd.

To my relief, I saw my mother's silhouette in the distance near the high hill. My bad dream about the slaughterhouse hadn't come true. There she was, alive, and standing next to two little colts. I whinnied loudly, "Look Stargazer, there's Mother standing on the hill with our new baby brothers by her side!"

My father had seen the trucks driving up the mountain and was ready to race off with my family, but he noticed horses jumping out of the van and running into the meadow. He turned towards us and ran down the hill to investigate.

He could not believe his eyes when he saw my sister. "Stargazer!" father yelled. He immediately chased her, the white mare, and the black filly back up the hill and into his group of mares.

My father was coming after me next. He started to charge at me. His eyes looked so angry. He pushed me and tried to bite my back. He even screamed at me to go away.

"Father, it's me! Wind! I've come home," I whinnied, as I tried to avoid his teeth and sharp hooves. He finally realized that I was his offspring, "Windy, my son, I thought you were gone forever. You've grown up." He paused, "I'll allow you to stay for the winter; someday you'll be a stallion with your own family and then you will have to leave. There can only be one stallion in this herd."

I felt bad things had changed, but I understood
my father's orders. In the wild, it's natural for the
youngsters to stay with their mothers until they're
breeding age. The mares continue to be part of the
band, but if they are males, the herd stallion will
eventually chase them out. Young males go off and
join bachelor gangs for safety from predators until
they can collect their own band of mares and defend
them from other stallions.

He reared up and commanded me, "But until then, I'm Silverado, and I'm in charge of this herd!" He chased me off to the right to test my strength and evaluate my position in the herd. I didn't fight with him, so he backed off. I would have to keep to the edge of the herd and not go near the mares like Rocket used to do. I lowered my head in submission and stepped to one side. I had to accept my rank in the herd in order to stay. "Yes, father, I'll stay out of your way. I've missed you and my family so much! I'm so glad to be home!"

I just wanted to run free!

In my excitement, I bolted up the hill where my mother stood. Her eyes were bright and so happy that Stargazer and I had returned to our family. "I can't believe what I'm seeing! I'm the luckiest mother in the world. All of my colts and fillies are here with me." She stamped her feet as if she was dancing. "This is the happiest day of my life." She kissed me softly on my forehead with her nose and welcomed my sister back with the same greeting.

For now, my family was safe and back together. I looked over my shoulder and saw Grampa and Emily waving. Then they got in the truck and started to drive away. Grampa had a big smile on his face and looked very pleased and proud that he had set us free. Emily was still crying, but she was smiling through her tears.

Grampa made a promise to drive back I the fall with a truckload of hay for the herd. He and Jim would make sure the water pump was working in the lower field and also keep track of the number of wild horses. The extra food and water he provided would help us survive the winter.

"I'm really free!" My heart started racing and I realized I was taller and stronger than when I was captured by the mustangers a year and a half ago. My brain felt like it was ready to explode with excitement and my whole body felt like an elastic band ready to snap. I leaped through the air and started running. I felt like I could run forever!

Big snowflakes began to fall lightly on my nose.
Mother was gazing proudly at my father who looked
like a magnificent statue on top of the hill. Suddenly, he
gave her a wink and shook his mane. Then he reared up
on his powerful hind legs and whinnied. "Run my family!
Run now! Far away from this road." He chased us up the
hill. I feel like my life is starting over. It's time to show my
father how fast I can gallop as we race the wind.

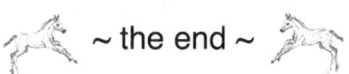 ~ the end ~

Why I wrote this story...

I grew up next to several horse farms in New Hampshire, took riding lessons, and have sketched and painted horses all my life. I was never able to have my own horse, but I have always had a soft spot in my heart for them. Being an equine artist has allowed me to stay in touch with horses and horse people. During my research about mustangs while writing this story, I discovered the troubling and haunting reality behind the capture and treatment of wild horses.

Each year, hundreds of thousands of wild mustangs and burros are being legally harvested, chased and harassed by mustangers and helicopter pilots; hot shotted, branded, and placed in holding pens with no shelter (often for years); and only given a few chances of adoption. If not adopted, they are sold and transported via crammed trailers across United States borders to slaughterhouses in Canada and Mexico. They are then killed and processed into horse meat which ends up in Europe and Japan for human consumption.

Some horses are poisoned by cattle ranchers, others are abused and neglected by owners who cannot take care of them due to a troubled economy. Rescue shelters and organizations across the country have joined the fight to help save them. However, stronger and stronger legislation and enforcement is needed to protect the wild mustangs and burros from terrible fates.

In a perfect world, the mustangs placed in the overcrowded holding pens would be vaccinated and immediately returned to the public lands to live free forever, just like in this story. However, the current laws do not offer this option. The multi-faceted slaughterhouse debate will continue until it is banned.

That is why I have joined the public outcry to rescue these horses from inhumane treatment and slaughter. I hope to educate people about the plight of the mustang and their potential elimination forever from public lands.

You can help, too. Share this story with your friends and family. Write a letter to your Congressman to vote to protect the horses from a slaughterhouse.

Volunteer at or donate to an animal rescue center, or adopt a wild horse or burro if you have a farm or ranch.

— Denise F. Brown,
   author, illustrator and horse admirer

You Can Help the Mustangs

To learn more about America's wild horses,
how they are being managed by man,
what's happening on the range and in Congress,
the risk of their extinction in the West,

and how the American public can help them survive

please visit:

www.windwildhorse.com